Anthropology, Government, History, Politics, Sociology

DAVID HAMMOND

TOM LESTER

JOE SCALES

DALE SEYMOUR PUBLICATIONS®

This book is published by Dale Seymour Publications®,
an imprint of Addison Wesley Longman, Inc.

Dale Seymour Publications
299 Jefferson Road
Parsippany, NJ 07054
Customer Service: 800-872-1100

Executive Editor: Catherine Anderson
Project Editor: Dorothy McDermott
Production/Manufacturing Director: Janet Yearian
Sr. Production/Manufacturing Coordinator: Fiona Santoianni
Design Director: Phyllis Aycock
Design Manager: Jeff Kelly
Text and Cover Design: Nita Ybarra Design
Composition and Computer Graphics: Eileen Sullivan

Copyright © 2000 by Dale Seymour Publications®. All rights reserved.
Printed in the United States of America

The publisher grants permission to individual teachers who have
purchased this book to reproduce the blackline masters as needed
for use with their own students. Reproduction for an entire school
or school district or for commercial use is prohibited.

ISBN 0-7690-0127-0
Order number 27304

1 2 3 4 5 6 7 8 9 10-ML-03 01 00 99

This Book Is Printed
On Recycled Paper

ACKNOWLEDGEMENTS
★

We would like to thank the *Sacramento Bee* for eighteen years of support by having a Plexer appear daily on the comic page. We appreciate the thousands of teachers and students who have made Plexers a part of their school programs, both as an academic tool and as a mind-expanding recreational pastime. We have published nearly 6,000 different Plexers. The encouragement to produce topical books came from subject matter teachers who through the years have asked, "Don't you have subject-centered Plexers that I can use with my students?" You are holding the result. We trust that we have met your expectations. To all of you Plexer fans, a big thank you!

David Hammond
Tom Lester
Joe Scales

INTRODUCTION

PLEXER is derived from the word *perplex* which means; "to confuse or puzzle; bewilder, to make confusedly intricate." It is the the prime objective of Plexer books to encourage students to think logically and to expand the ways in which they view the world and solve problems.

Divergent thinking is at the heart of Plexers. It gives students another communication code. Plexers allow them to try different solutions without risk, since there are no grades when solving Plexers. The possibility of developing an original piece of work is very high with Plexers. To invent something no one has ever seen before is very exciting.

Plexers are always associated with a Plexer box. The words and symbols placed in and around it stand for expressions, idioms, people, events, objects, and, in general, things that students are familiar with to some extent. The Plexer box gives license to use spelling and grammatical errors that are not acceptable in students' daily work. This has an appeal that motivates even the most precise student.

It is important that those who know the solution to a Plexer do not spoil the enjoyment of others discovering it on their own. An essential stage of problem solving, the "incubation stage," is rare in America's classrooms. Teachers are so used to "telling" and having closure that they forget students need to develop internal processes that advance data into a sequenced understanding. It is important to instruct for process as well as knowledge.

Using Social Studies Plexers in the Classroom.

- Social Studies is filled with persons, events, quotations, and places that lend themselves to Plexers. After students have had some experience solving the Plexers in this book they can create their own Plexers using topics they are currently studying or in which they have a special interest.

- Teachers may post a group of 2 or 3 Plexers on the bulletin board. At a convenient time of the day, ask students if they have a conjecture of what any of the Plexers mean. Difficult Plexers may stay on the board for a couple of days or longer. Invite students who have solved one or more of the Plexers to provide a new hint each day for those who have not.

- Include Plexers on worksheets, tests or quizzes as a last question or as a problem solving item. Some Plexers may have several solutions. Make a list of them and discuss the merits of each solution. There are no right or wrong answers. If the solution meets the Plexer's symbolism, it is acceptable.

*Plexers is a registered trademark of Plexers, Inc.

- Provide a page of Plexers to students. Have them work individually, in pairs, or in groups to solve the Plexers. Have students explain how they solved each Plexer. Use the discussion to refine problem solving strategies.

- Have students identify types of Plexers, giving samples of each type. For example, "location" could be one of the types. Under "location" students would include examples of the location of the Plexers in relation to the Plexer box: on the sides, down low, up high, in or out, in the middle, or even in corners. Students soon realize that location often becomes part of the solution for many of the Plexers.

- Use Plexers at the end of a class to keep minds occupied and promote mental development. Plexers also make good warm-up activities when returning to school after a long holiday.

- Have students choose their favorite Plexers and tell why they are favorites. This provides the students an opportunity to express their personal preferences for a variety of thought processes. Students will often choose one they created as their favorite, reinforcing the importance of being creative. Plexer creation is a form of creativity such as creative art, music and writing.

- As a general rule, the difficulty level of the Plexers increases from the beginning to the end of a page.

- Most importantly, Plexers are for fun! It is the authors' fondest wish that everyone enjoy the challenge of Plexers.

1 V V O O T T E E	2 *Gen der*	3 HE**R**O
4 −**LAKE**	5 + + +	6 A G E A G E
7 **AL↗C**	8 C(IT)²Y	9 N U FRONT FRONT FRONT

26. WAY / GET

27. (blank)

28. DONE

29. REPORT

29. ¢URY

30. UNIF↑ORM

31. ⨯ VAV ⨯

32. −C / NA

33. S T / PROGRESS / &

34. SUPENLA

35

TRAIL
L&

36

DAOR
DAOR

37

~~TAKE~~

PRIS
ER ER

38

BUTE
BUTE
BUTE

39

CHAIRO♀

40

UNCOM
VALOR

41

O　　S
　D u
　D u
O　　S

42

T
T + TR
T
T

43

WORL

44 RANK

45 MEX   ICO

46 B
LERT

47

PLEXERS — SOCIAL STUDIES

48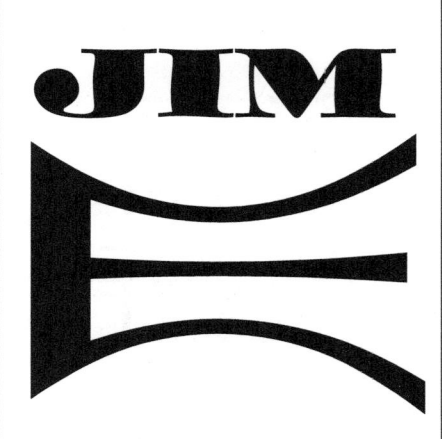

49

50 AGREEBBOT (with arrow up on final T)

51 QUE On

52
LAKE　TARIO

53
T E
　NING
STREET

54
N E Z I T I C (vertical)

55
D –

56
(blank)

57
I　E
　L
I　E

(vertical: B L O O K in square 56 right side)

58
$\dfrac{HEAD}{4}$ $\dfrac{HEAD}{4}$

59
8 (with PROC / RAST inside)

60
NAH$_2$OTIONH$_2$OAL

61 FIRE COURAGE	**62** ¢US	**63** F I R E CHAT CHAT CHAT F I R E
64 ST(R)EET	**65** PRIN^B_BT	**66** SUROLLS
67 DENOED	**68** G&HI	**69** COODO

70. BIG WIG

71. GOVERNMENT OVERTHROWN

72. POLE VAULTING (POLE's with missing middle)

73. NORTHWEST PASSAGE

74. SENATE (SEN-8)

75. POINT OF ORIGIN

76. NEW ZEALAND

77. EXPLORER

78

B
I
L
L

79

J
U
R
Y

80

TRAINING
JOB

81

A E
★ ★ ★ ★

(Plexers logo: SOCIAL STUDIES PLEXERS)

82

GR8
LAKE
LAKE

83

N
•   E
S

84

FAVLOLR
 ‾ ‾ ‾

85

MAYFLOWER

10

86. TRAFALGAR²

87. GROUND / RR

88. SPHERE (arched)

89. TRESS / TRESS / TRESS / TRESS

SOCIAL STUDIES PLEXERS®

90. LIBERATIO♀

91. SAILED / CCCCCCC

92. ⚔ / LAW

93. & OZ O↑T

94 G N I S I R	95 	96 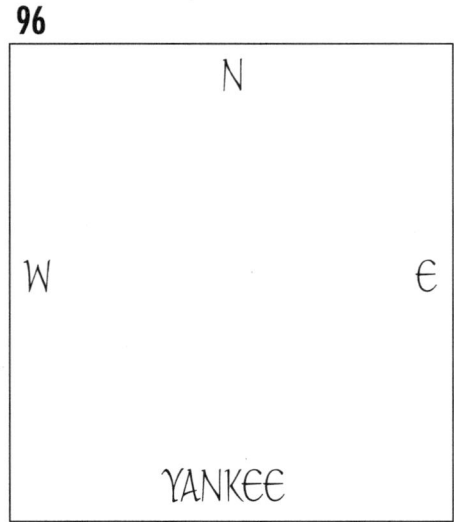
97 	98 	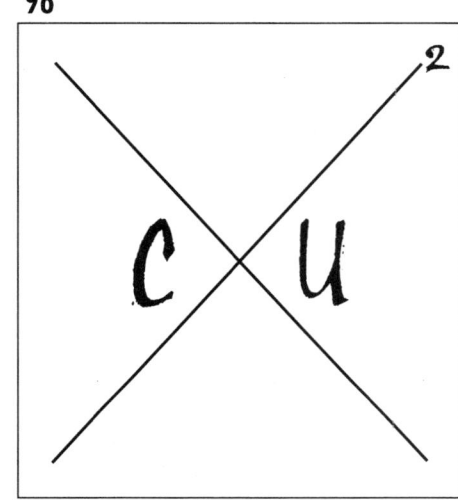
99 	100 	101 **VADHUNSING**

102

103 C H O I C E (vertical)

104 PHRASE / PHRASE

105 TEERTS JUSTICE

P S Y C H (vertical)

SOCIAL STUDIES PLEXERS

★ ★ ★ ★
PA 2,000 lb

107
```
I O N A T I
O N A T I O
N A T I O N
A T I O N A
T I O N A T
I O N A T I
O N A T I T
```

108 G̶U̶T̶S̶ / G̶L̶O̶R̶Y̶

109 AODOT (with arrows on O's)

110	111	112
JACKED JET	I S T	JUSTICE JUSTICE JUSTICE JUSTICE

113	114	115
E ATEXAMION A M	H.I.S.T.O.R.Y.	90's ☺

116	117	118
= PAY = = = = WORK	NUVO$	

119 WALK MOON	**120** ♂HATTAN	**121** ROCK
122 M☾N	**123** SOCIAL STUDIES PLE✗ERS	**123** G O
124 	**125** Ab & SHIP	**126** 20 20 20 20 & 7 YEARS AGO R FATHER FATHER FATHER FATHER

145 ccccc	**146** gROUND	**147** T O W N
148 G E T BRASSBRASS TACKS	SOCIAL STUDIES PLEX ERS	**150** WELCOME AR MS
151 O N E	**152** BALLOON	**153** ★ STATE

153
POINT (curved/bent)

154
AN
ATL TIC

155
60" O↗

156
T R I U M P H (arched)

157
P P
R R
E
S S
S S
LAND

158
MOON (fading)

159
COCUURT

160
$\frac{FRENCH}{4}$

161
VERSITY + VERSITY
COMING

162 WING	**163** AIL	**164** FALSE COLORS SAIL
165 PONY PRESS PRESS	**166** BÓNDING	**167** R R
168 D	**169** e ago	**170** ROO EM PIRE

171	172	173
Green Green (reflected)	mmmm	dog 4the (upside down)

174	175
:ii	SOCIAL STUDIES PLEXERS
	TIC TIC TIC TIC TIC TIC TIC TIC TIC TIC TIC TIC

176	177	178
R RED D	COURT (notch)	SETTLES •—O

188	189	190
weSTWARD	AMEMADERICA	MIRAL + MIRAL

191	192	193
CALIBUR / CALIBUR / CALIBUR	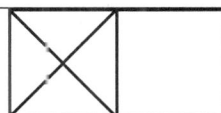 Au	NOITANIMIRCSID

194	195	196
	effGOect / effGOect	4D

197. WORLD / FIRE

198. HIS W⬆RD

199. F E L / ⠀E

200. GET THE / THE •

201. HORSE ¢

202. NEWS (broken)

203. ♡ L &

204. CALIFORNIA (slanting down)

205. STOP 0

215

216

217

218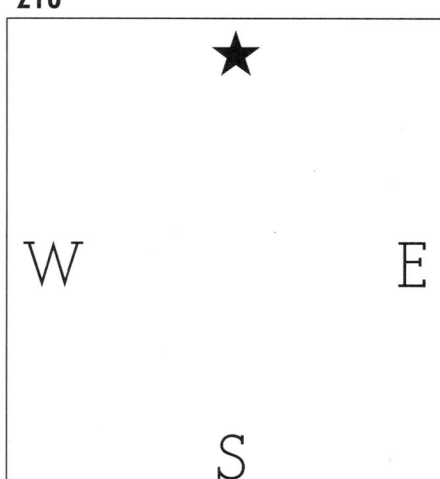

219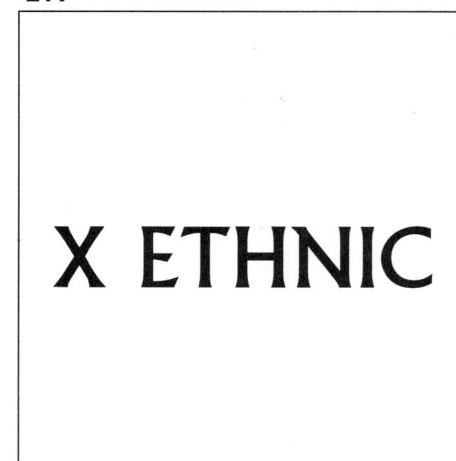

220

221

222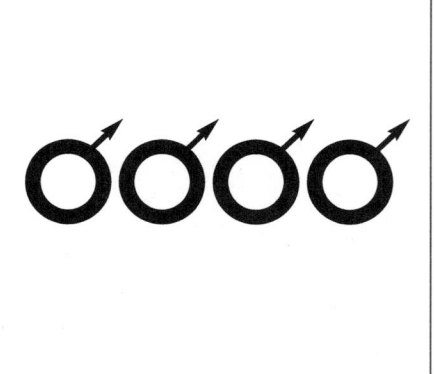

223	224	225
HOME−	SEA SON	E T A D NEWS

226	227	228
COM O↗ (O with arrow)	⇑ PUNISH O↗T	L & FLING

229	230	231
ST⃫ONE	═DDDDDDD═	WAi**HOUSE**

232

HA

233

WAR (upside down)

234

CREDIB   ILITY

235

c

236

COM
  ¢

237

CADE

238

CTORGANVIETLO

239

O°

240

MOTION
RULED

241

VOTE
DAY
DAY

242

it + it

243

D'

244

C
A
S
EV T IL
L
E

245

COHOUSINGME

246

B
WAR

247

EVIDENT
(circles below)

248

TR8R

249

B
A
R

250

YPS

251

LAW
=

252

MERCY

W
I
T
H

253

CAJUSTSE

254

EN
EN
EN
EN

CORRESP
DENT

255

W
I
N
L
A
N
D

256

INDUSTRIAL (upside down)

257

FI　　RE

258

NOSEWIN

259

SCENIC
LOOK

260

C

261

NOROD

262

CAN O E
TYLER
TYLER

263

SOCIETY

264

UNITED　　E
　　　　　　W
　　　　　　W
　÷　　　　W
　　　　　　E

265	**266**	**267**
LAW –	YGOLOHCYSP	⊘¢
268	**269**	**270**
IF L &	SCHSTAYOOL	VICIL
271	**272**	**273**
B♪K	SOCIAL (diagonal)	CRISIS / LIFE (crossed)

ANSWERS
★

page 1

1. the right to vote
2. gender gap
3. fallen hero
4. bottomless lake
5. triad
6. the Middle Ages
7. almanac
8. city square center
9. new frontiers

page 2

10. labor of love
11. put to sea
12. Undersecretary of State
13. assumption
14. back him up
15. north to Alaska
16. Germany
17. Tripoli

page 3

18. take sides
19. absentee ballot
20. the right to remain silent
21. small claims court
22. Samuel Adams
23. Calcutta
24. army surplus
25. piracy or pie rack

page 4

26. get underway
27. outdone
28. full report
29. turn of the century
30. man or men in uniform
31. not half bad
32. Barcelona (bar c low na)
33. stand in the way of progress
34. peninsula

page 5

35. Overland Trail
36. back roads
37. take no prisoners
38. tribute
39. chairwomen or chairwoman
40. uncommon valor
41. exodus
42. Fort Sumter
43. world without end

page 6

44. rank high
45. Gulf of Mexico
46. be on the alert
47. Bering Sea ("bare" ing)
48. Jim Bowie
49. no discrimination
50. to be in agreement
51. It's out of the question

page 7

52. Lake Ontario
53. Ten Downing Street
54. upright citizen
55. debar
56. be on the lookout
57. exile
58. headquarters
59. procrastinate
60. international waters

page 8

61. courage under fire
62. census
63. fireside chats (FDR's method)
64. our man in the street
65. to be out of print
66. the Dead Sea Scrolls
67. no indeed
68. Gandhi
69. commando

page 9

70. a big wig (VIP)
71. government overthrown
72. poles apart
73. Northwest Passage
74. Senate
75. point of origin
76. New Zealand
77. role reversal

page 10

78. Bill of Right(s)
79. the jury is out
80. on the job training
81. attorney general
82. Great Lakes
83. West Point
84. All in favor
85. Mayflower Compact

page 11

86. Trafalgar Square
87. underground railroad
88. hemisphere
89. fortress
90. women's liberation
91. sailed across the seven seas
92. no one is above the law
93. announcement

page 12

94. uprising
95. paratroopers
96. Southern Yankee
97. silver star
98. see you in times square
99. fall into the trap
100. midshipman
101. invading Huns

page 13

102. right choice
103. paraphrase
104. back street justice
105. psych out (on to someone)
106. General Patton
107. United Nations
108. no guts, no glory
109. amendment

page 14

110. hijacked jet
111. leftist
112. out for justice
113. cross examination
114. periods of history
115. Gay Nineties
116. equal pay for equal work
117. nouveau riche
118. Latino

page 15

119. walk on the moon
120. Manhattan

121. Little Rock (AR)
122. monarch
123. Fargo (ND)
124. Nome, Alaska
125. abandon ship
126. "Fourscore and seven......."

page 16

127. on the spot reporter
128. civil right
129. "...two if by sea..."
130. division of labor
131. open question
132. middle of the road stance
133. Portland (nautical left)
134. Delhi (India)
135. amend

page 17

136. split ticket
137. nomad
138. topic
139. above average I. Q.
140. south seas
141. overnight journey
142. Minneapolis
143. countryside
144. the lesser of two evils

page 18

145. the high seas
146. groundswell
147. downtown
148. get down to brass tacks
149. welcome with open arms
150. one sided
151. trial balloon (tri-L)
152. Lone Star State (Texas)

page 19

153. turning point
154. mid-atlantic ridge
155. minuteman
156. Arch of Triumph
157. Overland Express
158. Half Moon (Henry Hudson's ship)
159. see you in court
160. French Quarter
161. overcoming adversity

page 20

162. left wing
163. cut off aid
164. sail under false colors
165. Pony Express
166. male bonding
167. tours
168. deport (left d)
169. eon ago
170. decline and fall of the Roman Empire

page 21

171. greenbacks
172. forum
173. for the underdog
174. colonize
175. politics (poly-tics)
176. Red Cross
177. settle out of court
178. Point Barrow (Alaska)

page 22

179. undercover policeman or undercover cop
180. war between North and South

181. good times
182. diplomat
183. Paris
184. "A house divided..."
185. ill-starred exploit
186. Cuba
187. foreign intrigue

page 23

188. westward expansion
189. made in America
190. admirals
191. Excalibur (King Arthur's sword)
192. gold strike
193. reverse discrimination
194. Manitoba
195. go into effect
196. Ford (Henry)

page 24

197. set the world on fire
198. man of his word
199. felony
200. get to the point
201. horse sense
202. news breaking
203. heartland
204. lower California
205. stop at nothing

page 25

206. nationwide
207. out to sea
208. no man's land
209. essay
210. War of the Roses (row "s"es)
211. criminal
212. whitewash
213. westward
214. Iron Age

page 26

215. mandate
216. Niagara Falls
217. national forest
218. north star
219. multiethnic
220. barbarian
221. Harry S. Truman
222. Roman or foremen

page 27

223. homeless
224. open season
225. update on the news
226. common man
227. corporal punishment
228. highland fling
229. cornerstone
230. defense
231. halfway house

page 28

232. aloha
233. war is over
234. credibility gap
235. Ceylon (c lone)
236. <u>Common Sense</u> (written by Thomas Paine)
237. blockade
238. travel incognito
239. Ohio
240. motion overruled

page 29

241. vote today

242. summit
243. defeat ("D" feet)
244. medieval castle
245. low-income housing
246. Beyond War
247. evident in the highest circles
248. traitor

page 30

249. side bar
250. counter spy
251. equal under the law
252. without mercy
253. just in case
254. foreign correspondent
255. win by a landslide
256. industrial revolution

page 31

257. open fire!
258. win by a nose
259. scenic overlook
260. seaport (c left)
261. Normandy
262. "Tippecanoe and Tyler too"
263. high society
264. "United we stand, divided we fall."

page 32

265. lawless
266. reverse psychology
267. innocent
268. "One if by land..."
269. stay in school
270. civil disorder
271. notebook
272. social climber
273. mid-life crisis